GENEROSITY

How God's Radical Grace Changes Our Perspective on Money and Possessions

GENEROSITY

How God's Radical Grace Changes Our Perspective on Money and Possessions

"...Everything comes from you, and we have given you only what comes from your hand."

I Chronicles 29:14

A 20-Day Devotional by Andrew Field & Redeemer Presbyterian Church

gospel in life

*Generosity: How God's Radical Grace Changes Our Perspective
on Money and Possessions*

Copyright © 2016 by Redeemer Presbyterian Church, located
at 1166 Avenue of the Americas, 16th floor, New York, NY 10036.
Previously printed under the title "A 20-Day Study in Stewardship."

ISBN-13: 978-1-944549-01-5

Scripture taken from the HOLY BIBLE, TODAY'S NEW INTERNATIONAL
VERSION®. TNIV®. Copyright © 2001,
2005 by International Bible Society. All rights reserved.

*Generosity: How God's Radical Grace Changes Our Perspective
on Money and Possessions* was written by Rev. Andrew Field while he
was a pastor at Redeemer Presbyterian Church of New York City.

Cover and interior design: Lee Marcum

Printed in the United States of America

CONTENTS

HOW TO USE THIS DEVOTIONAL

This guide provides 20 daily readings, each exploring
God's call to Christians to become stewards of his bountiful
provision. They are intended to encourage us, to rebuke us
sometimes, and to instruct us.

Money is a sensitive issue in our culture. And yet it is central to
our commitment to Jesus Christ and a yardstick to measure our
understanding of grace.

The purpose of this devotion is to explore the wide range of
biblical teaching about our heart's attachment to the treasures
of this world. Experience why Christian giving is such an
adventure. Most of all, renew your heart and change your life,
by soaking in the gospel hope which motivates us to live for
his glory and to care for others.

Each day's reading has four parts. Expect to spend 20 minutes
reading, meditating and praying. Another, perhaps even better,
way to cover this material is to team up with a trusted friend
or a fellowship group. Discuss each day what you have learned
and help each other apply the lessons.

❍ Read
   Slowly read the passage listed. The passages are relatively
   short, so take time to consider each phrase. If you do not
   understand something, you might refer to your Bible's study
   notes.

❍ Apply
   Ponder the brief interpretation in light of the passage. What
   is the biblical writer trying to say? What is the main point?
   Using the thought-provoking questions, seek the Spirit's
   guidance regarding your own response to the passage. These

are not quick fill-in-the-blank questions; they are intended to cause you to slow down and meditate on the truth God is teaching you. How does the biblical teaching apply to your life? Where do you need to grow or change? How has Christ already changed you?

❍ *Pray*

Pray for a genuinely transformed life that models Christ's life. You might use this time to pray for other issues as well. Praise Christ for his goodness.

❍ *Do*

Daily suggestions that help drive the message in practical ways deep into your heart and life.

DAY 1
YOUR ONLY TRUE TREASURE

For where your treasure is, there your heart will be also.

—Matthew 6:21

● *Read*
See Matthew 6:21 printed above.

● *Apply*
Jesus here tells us the most important lesson about money. Our heart, our desire and hope, is tied closely to our treasure. Our money and our heart go together. We all know that, of course, to some extent. But when Jesus calls our attention to this part of our character, he confronts us.

He alerts us to the powerful tug that material wealth possesses, an allure that makes us do and act and believe contrary to our Christian confession. We say that we live for heaven. Our pocketbook shows us what we really live for. He calls us to examine where we place our money and our heart: earthly pleasures that fade away or eternal kingdom investments that last forever.

1. Where is most of your treasure? Is that where your heart is?

2. When you give, does that frighten you or excite you? Why?

◗ *Pray*

For a renewed heart that tells treasure what to do, not more treasure that tells your heart what to do.

◗ *Do*

Look at your bank statement and your credit card statements. Specifically, where does most of your money go? Are those your priorities?

DAY 2
GOD'S OWNERSHIP OF CREATION

You may say to yourself, "My power and the strength of my hands have produced this wealth for me." But remember the Lord your God, for it is he who gives you the ability to produce wealth.

—Deuteronomy 8:17-18a

◗ Read
Psalm 50, especially verses 7-15.

◗ Apply
God is the creator (Genesis 1:1), the sole ruler and Lord over all creation. He controls all things in this world, the whole creation (Psalm 50:12). Nothing that we do takes away from God's overruling presence throughout all of creation. It is his to create, and protect, and use for his glory. So whenever we use the resources of the world, we use the resources of God's world.

That also means that "the silver is mine and the gold is mine" (Haggai 2:8). When we look at our own finances, we tend to forget God's sovereign ownership of creation. We expect him to care for us as if he owes us something. In Job 41:11, God replies, "Who has a claim against me that I must pay? Everything under heaven belongs to me." Or, we think that we have earned our treasures because of our own abilities (see Deuteronomy 8:17 above).

Therefore, God doesn't need our money as if he needed an income. Instead, we need him every moment to sustain us. Our worship, and the dedication of our whole lives to him, is an acknowledgment of his control over everything. It's a thank offering, a giving back of what we have so abundantly received (Psalm 50:14).

1. Do you act like God "owes" you something? Why?

2. What causes you to forget God's loving control of the world?

❍ Pray

For a renewed heart that daily remembers God's active control of the world and a thankful heart that praises his loving care.

❍ Do

How might living as if God owns everything influence the way we shop, the presents we put under the Christmas tree, the vacations we plan, our giving to the needy? [1]

DAY 3
GOD'S OWNERSHIP OF HIS PEOPLE

For who makes you different from anyone else? What do you have that you did not receive? And if you did receive it, why do you boast as though you did not?

—1 Corinthians 4:7

❍ **Read**
See 1 Corinthians 4:7-14.

❍ **Apply**
Everything good in our lives comes from God: our abilities, our upbringing, our educational background. We would not be where we are without countless interventions by God on our behalf. Beyond those temporary blessings, God has given his children the greatest gift of all: his only son. The Corinthian church, and many of us today, practically ignore the full wonder of that claim.

The gospel is a gift. Our union with Christ is all by God's grace. There is nothing we did to deserve it or earn it. In fact, we all were in rebellion against God (Romans 1:18ff, 3:23). And yet Christ died for his people, bearing their sin and giving them his righteousness (2 Corinthians 5:21). When we forget that, according to Paul, we become prideful and selfish.

What if someone loaned us $100,000? Would we resent giving them five dollars? Would we treat all those resources as ours alone? God gives us things of this world to use on his behalf.

He didn't have to. But we are his children now, he loves us and gives us what we need and what we can employ to further his kingdom, to spread his grace even more. His goodness includes giving us the joy of commitment to him.

1. **Would you treat your things differently if they belonged to someone else? What if you acted as if God owned everything you have: your home, your clothes, your furniture, your money, your time?**

2. **What have you received from God? How is your life different because of Christ?**

○ *Pray*
Pray for a renewed, joyful heart, using the words of Psalm 100. "Know that the Lord is good. It is he who made us, and we are his; we are his people, the sheep of his pasture."

○ *Do*
Think of ten big purchases that you've made in the past year or so. Discretely (or even just mentally) label them "Provided By and Belonging to God. For His Use Only." [2]

DAY 4
TRUE SECURITY

*"If I have put my trust in gold
 or said to pure gold, 'You are my security.'"*

—Job 31:24

○ *Read*
Luke 12:13-21

○ *Apply*
The rich fool thought that he could trust in his grain. Yet the grain outlasted his own life. He invested his wealth with something it could not give: security. It would always be there to make his life comfortable. But the things of this world are unstable, a pile of sand ready to collapse. God's response to him is blunt: "You fool."

"Having lots of money can be like a drug. It can make you feel powerful and giddy. It can convince you that everything is going to be okay." [3] We think that only if we accumulate more and more will we have enough. That day never comes-"enough" is never reached. When we trust our Lord we can stop hoarding wealth beyond our needs and become "rich toward God."

The only true security comes from trusting in God's care for his children. As Christians, we can be assured that God loves us because of Christ's work on our behalf. Therefore, we can loosen our grip on our treasures. We see them as temporary and God's kingdom as eternal.

1. How much money do you want left when you die? Why?

2. What does becoming "rich toward God" look like? Does that reflect your own lifestyle? Why or why not?

Pray

Pray for a renewed heart that treats money as a mere thing, and treats God as the only true security.

Do

Look at your long-term goals: home, retirement, children. How much accumulation of wealth is required to meet those goals? What if your lifestyle was greatly simplified—how much less would you need? Would you give away the difference?

DAY 5
WHO DO WE WORSHIP?

No one can serve two masters. Either you will hate the one and love the other, or you will be devoted to the one and despise the other. You cannot serve both God and money.

Therefore I tell you, do not worry about your life, what you will eat or drink; or about your body, what you will wear. Is not life more than food, and the body more than clothes?

—Matthew 6:24-25

❯ Read
Matthew 6:24-34

❯ Apply
Jesus personifies wealth as Mammon. He even gives it the status of a false God, an idol, and lays down an all-or-nothing claim: if you worship wealth, you won't worship God. Our heart cannot contain two masters, two gods.

Worry is an indicator of worship. What you worry about is what you don't want to lose. Therefore, Jesus says that worrying about money and your future is an indicator of a lack of trust in God. Worse, it shows that the heart's true hope is in wealth. "His words are so uncomfortable that even those of us who say we love him and fight to defend Scripture's authority find ourselves looking for ways around what he says." [4]

Research has shown that many people do not give because they are afraid. [5] The only way to ever stop worrying about money is to break its stranglehold on your heart by becoming generous. When you give money away, you stop worshipping it.

1. If you gave until it lowered your lifestyle, would you be worried? Of what?

2. What would you give up to become enormously rich? Would you give up friends and family? Would you give up your time? Christ? What would you give up just to be "comfortable"?

○ *Pray*

Pray for a renewed heart that worships Christ alone and rejects the idol of Mammon.

○ *Do*

Catch yourself worshipping money—daydreaming or worrying about it. Worship Christ instead using the same loving terms: "If I only had more of Jesus...", "With more of Christ in my life we could...", "I hope my new job gives me plenty of time to serve Jesus..." etc.

DAY 6
CONTENTMENT

Keep your lives free from the love of money and be content with what you have, because God has said,

> *"Never will I leave you;*
> *never will I forsake you."*

—Hebrews 13:5

⊙ *Read*
Hebrews 13:1-6

⊙ *Apply*
In the midst of exhorting Christians to live according to the gospel, the writer to the Hebrews actually commands contentment. Just as contentment is a result of trusting God, it is also the *means* of trusting God. To be discontent is to accuse God of being either unloving or impotent. Contentment with our life is therefore as important a virtue as love, hospitality, mercy, or fidelity.

Sadly, we live in a culture of discontent. Every day we see an average of 3,500 ads, each trying to convince us that what we have is not good enough. [6] We need something new, something better, something more fashionable. Desires become hopes, which become wants, which become "needs." "I've just got to have that new HDTV wide-screen TV." Once the newness wears off, it's time for another new thing.

Paul advises Timothy to stay focused on the lasting joy of contentment. "But godliness with contentment is great gain. For we brought nothing into the world, and we can take nothing out of it." (1 Timothy 6:6)

1. Are you content with what you have? If not, then why not?

2. How do you handle the pressure to "keep up" or conform to a higher standard of living?

> **Pray**
> For a renewed heart that is content with God's provision, that isn't always looking to new things for satisfaction.

> **Do**
> Carefully look at a few ads today. What type of "salvation" or "better life" do they promise (approval, peace of mind, comfort, prestige, etc.)? How do they entice people into thinking that their life isn't good enough without this thing?

DAY 7
MONEY AT THE ROOT

For the love of money is a root of all kinds of evil.

—1 Timothy 6:10a

❍ *Read*
1 Timothy 6:6-10

❍ *Apply*
This famous passage is central to our view of money. Paul claims that money is at the bottom of a wide variety of sin and idolatry. Money is like a spice in the smorgasbord of sinful desires. In other words, few people lust after mere dollar bills. Instead, money plays into idolatries of security, comfort, approval, or power. We like money because it gets us something we want. Even the Scrooge, always counting his coins, is actually counting his security, counting the thing he trusts in rather than God.

The warning flags are up. As a Christian, we are free to use money, but we should use it with caution, understanding its dangerous ability to turn our hearts from Christ to the things of this world. Jesus goes so far as to call Mammon "unrighteous" (Luke 16:9). [7] "We so badly want to believe that mammon has no power over us, no authority of its own. But by giving the descriptive *unrighteous* to mammon, Jesus forbids us from ever taking so naive a view of wealth. We must be more tough minded, more realistic." [8]

1. Take an honest look at some of your most intense desires. Does money play a role in them? In what way does it play a role?

2. What do you think about people who have a lot more money and possessions than you do? Are they better people, more secure, live a better life?

○ *Pray*

Pray for a renewed heart that recognizes the power of money to turn your desires away from Christ and is able to counter that power by remembering the beauty of Christ.

○ *Do*

Take one alluring aspect of money and write a list of the ways it affects your life. For example, "The ways that I act like money gives me pleasure are..." or "The ways that I act like money makes me better than other people are..."

DAY 8
THE ANTIDOTE

*Command them to do good, to be rich in good deeds, and
to be generous and willing to share.*

—1 Timothy 6:18

○ *Read*
1 Timothy 6:6-9, 17-19

○ *Apply*
Paul has already warned us about the dangerous side of
money in this passage. He now turns to the biblical use of
money, by urging Timothy to teach the rich in Ephesus to
invest their treasure into eternal purposes. The purpose of
wealth is to do good with it. What a noble and high calling.
Note that he doesn't command the rich to become poor.
Instead he commands the rich to be generous, "rich in good
deeds." They give up one type of riches to gain another. And
in doing that, they break the enslaving grip that treasures
have on our heart.

In short, the antidote for money's poisonous effect in our
lives is generosity. It's an antidote of drinking the sweet
medicine of trusting in God's control of the future, trusting
in the "life that is truly life." This is first of all a generosity
of the heart. The heart has to turn to loving good deeds
more than loving riches. This is a significant turning. And it
is a quantifiable turning—when money actually leaves the
account and goes to God's kingdom.

1. John Newton's method was to figure out what a "barely decent" lifestyle was (home, food, clothing), and then to give one penny away for every penny spent on oneself. What would your life be like if you followed that method?

2. In what areas do you most struggle with being content? Consider the areas of possessions, career advancement, home life, children's accomplishments, to name a few. How would the antidote of being "rich in good deeds" help combat our natural disposition toward being discontent?

○ *Pray*
Pray for courage to fight the good fight of faith in the area of contentment. Pray for yourself and your family, that you would be energized by the "good deeds" that can be done through generous giving.

○ *Do*
Make a list of the charitable organizations that are doing good deeds in your community. Reach out to a few of these organizations to see what tangible needs they have. Give gifts to them, both monetary and volunteer time, to help meet these needs.

DAY 9
THE MOTIVE

I am not commanding you, but I want to test the sincerity of your love by comparing it with the earnestness of others. For you know the grace of our Lord Jesus Christ, that though he was rich, yet for your sake he became poor, so that you through his poverty might become rich.

—2 Corinthians 8:8-9

❍ Read
2 Corinthians 8:1-15

❍ Apply
In one of the first recorded church fundraising letters in history, Paul appealed to one single motive for giving: the grace of Christ. Christians don't give because they should (although they do) or because it frees their life from the idolatry of Mammon (although it does).

Christians give because they know that God gave everything, even his own son Jesus Christ, for their sakes. Grace is the motivation for giving. Giving is a response to a gift of sheer grace. Just as those who are forgiven much also forgive, those who have been given much (peace with God, eternal life, the love of Christ, the indwelling Spirit, and more) give in return.

The Macedonians understood that grace so much that even in the midst of their own difficult circumstances they happily gave beyond their ability (8:1-4). They begged to give more.

1. Do you beg God to be able to give more than you do now?
   What is your goal?

2. What typically motivates your giving? Guilt, duty, expecta-
   tion of God's blessing or thankfulness?

O *Pray*

Pray for a renewed lifestyle that places a priority on giving.

O *Do*

Give away some cash (not a check) this week simply because
you love Jesus. Don't let anyone know about it or claim it on
your taxes.

DAY 10
A CHEERFUL GIVER

*Each of you should give what you have decided in your heart
to give, not reluctantly or under compulsion, for God loves a
cheerful giver.*

—2 Corinthians 9:7

○ Read
2 Corinthians 9:6-15

○ Apply
When Christians give, as we saw yesterday, they give
motivated by grace. A reluctant gift or a guilt-manipulated
gift is not generosity. It's paying a "God tax," it's fulfilling an
obligation.

A generous lifestyle, however, is a life of freedom, of
simplicity, of joy, of fruitfulness, of purpose. There is a
satisfaction to pleasing God, to bringing joy and honor to
him.

A Christian should smile as they give, they should want
to give. We should see giving like a roller coaster ride: it
feels adventurous and risky, but it's really safe. We think
we are going to plummet, but God holds onto us tightly
(9:8). Anything that much fun becomes contagious. Many
Christians experience that thrill; once they make giving a
priority, it becomes more and more joyful.

1. **Is giving money away fun for you? If yes, then when did that joy begin? If not, then why not?**

2. **Do you desire to give more than you do now (see yesterday's passage)? What stops you from giving?**

◉ *Pray*

Pray for a renewed lifestyle that expresses grace, that holds onto possessions loosely, that finds joy in giving.

◉ *Do*

As you give, either on Sunday or at another time, use the act of giving as a specific act of worship.

DAY 11
STARTING SOMEWHERE

A tithe of everything…belongs to the Lord.

—Leviticus 27:30

○ Read
Leviticus 27:30-33

○ Apply
In the Old Testament, all believers were required to give a tenth of income to God's work and the poor. The tithe is still a minimum guideline for our giving.

The tithe (or ten percent) guideline makes many Christians feel guilty. Some of that guilt, as we saw yesterday, is false. However, as one observer states: "…some of us should feel legitimately guilty about what we put in the offering plate. Relative to the wealth that has been placed in our care, few of us give sacrificially. We are greedy and giving God the leftovers. The law has a legitimate role to bring us to the righteous God at the foot of the cross, where we meet a gracious loving Christ. It is the love of Christ that we are responding to, that motivates us to be great givers and deep lovers."[9]

What about grace? The tithe is not a law that brings us merit in God's eyes. It shows us that we need the grace of Christ to cover our greed, to set us free from self-service.

We then can see the tithe just like every other law of God as a means of expressing gratitude. That's what Leviticus says the tithe was for anyway.

1. **Do you tithe your income? Do you give away more than ten percent, or less?**

2. **What would it take to move your giving up one level, giving away a few percent more next year?**

○ *Pray*

Pray for a renewed lifestyle that moves up each year in giving to biblical proportions, from nothing to tithing to beyond.

○ *Do*

What is your income level? What is ten percent of the gross? How does that compare to your giving?

DAY 12
PROPORTION

On the first day of every week, each one of you should set aside a sum of money in keeping with your income.

—1 Corinthians 16:2a

⊙ Read
1 Corinthians 15:58-16:4

⊙ Apply
After a lengthy discussion of the glories of resurrection in Christ, Paul places an important "therefore" in 15:58. Because we know for sure that death is defeated at the cross, we can fearlessly stand firm in faith and move out in ministry into the world.

When we worship, we respond to the hope of the gospel by committing our lives to the wonderful God that we believe in. Worship is, in short, giving. To worship, we must not only give him our praise, our attention, our sins, our fears, our burdens, and our hearts, but also our money.

So Paul advised the Corinthians to offer their gifts as an act of worship "on the first day of the week" (Sunday). This regular, planned offering ensured not only the right proportion of generosity, but also that the gifts were used as a joyful, praise-filled response to grace. For that reason, Christians have always seen regular Sunday offerings as a normal means of giving.

1. Do you give each week just to "pay for your seat" at church or to worship?

_____

2. Is your giving regular or sporadic? How would regular giving increase both the proportion and the joy of generosity?

_____

❍ Pray

Pray for a lifestyle of consistent, regular giving to the Lord what he has called you to give.

❍ Do

Take the amount that you feel God calls you to give and divide it by 12 (monthly) or 52 (weekly). Commit to giving that regular amount at worship, doubling on weeks you may be out of town. Giving by check instead of cash helps keep a record of consistency. (For self-employed freelance people, you may need to base giving on whenever income arrives rather than a set weekly amount).

DAY 13
INVESTING IN THE KINGDOM

Sell your possessions and give to the poor. Provide purses for yourselves that will not wear out, a treasure in heaven that will never fail, where no thief comes near and no moth destroys.

—Luke 12:33

◐ Read
Luke 12:22-34

◐ Apply
Only two things from this world will never pass away: God's Word and people. When we invest our resources into people, we are making an eternal decision. Jesus tells us that giving cannot be a losing investment.

Are you spending on things that will pass away, or investing in a cause that will make a difference forever? As the hymn writer John Newton puts it: "Fading is the worldlings pleasure, all his boasted pomp and show / Solid joys and lasting treasure, none but Zion's children know." God's kingdom will never end, billions of years after every "safe" investment on earth has disintegrated. Giving money to the poor, according to Jesus, is not throwing money away; rather, it is the only reasonable thing to do.

1. What do you consider "safe" in this world? How does that compare to the safety of God's eternal kingdom?

2. Do you have the same concern for the poor as Jesus did? Why or why not?

❍ *Pray*

Pray for a renewed lifestyle that sees people as more eternal than things and thereby puts more effort, time and money into people for the sake of Jesus Christ.

❍ *Do*

Find a person that you know that has a practical need. Try to meet (at least part of) that need by getting rid of something that you have. Don't give away something worn out; give away something you like.

DAY 14
SACRIFICE OF FIRST FRUITS

For I testify that they gave as much as they were able,
and even beyond their ability. Entirely on their own...

—2 Corinthians 8:3

◗ Read
Deuteronomy 26:1-4, 9-11

◗ Apply
The idea of "first fruits" giving is to offer up to God the first
rewards of our labor in acknowledgment that what we have
is a gift from God. The first fruits were the choicest, the best
of the harvest. The Israelites were saying, "God, you've
given us this bounty, so now we give it back to you."

Giving the first fruits is also a sacrifice. They could be sold
for a higher price than the rest of the harvest. In giving them
away, God's people trusted him to provide a continued
harvest. It was therefore a sacrificial pledge; a promise that
all things belong to God.

Christ gave sacrificially, and so Christian giving is sacrificial
giving. His first fruits were the pledge of the Holy Spirit,
the guarantee of the full harvest of his promise. Christians
have always continued this practice, giving "off the top"
sacrificially, trusting that the Lord will provide.

1. What would be the "first fruits" of your life: your pre-tax income, your investments, your time, your abilities, your "earning potential"? How are those a gift from God?

2. What kind of a plan could you create to give first to God in everything?

❯ *Pray*

Pray for a renewed lifestyle that seeks to give God the first of everything in all areas of life.

❯ *Do*

How could you encourage other Christians to help each other give first to God? How could our church community do that?

DAY 15
OUTGIVING GOD

"Bring the whole tithe into the storehouse, that there may be food in my house. Test me in this," says the Lord Almighty, "and see if I will not throw open the floodgates of heaven and pour out so much blessing that there will not be room enough to store it..."

—Malachi 3:10

❍ Read
Malachi 3:8-12

❍ Apply
God dares you to trust him in giving. He doesn't simply command obedience. He shows us how wildly generous he is, how quick to give out his favor. Then he says: if you belong to me, do likewise. Giving is an adventure that is rewarding beyond your wildest dreams. The joy of trust flows into every area of our life: from finances, to career, to the future, to relationships, to hard times. When we live according to our solid grasp of God's goodness, our whole lives are more free and steadfast. We gain a courage that can withstand trials when we believe that Jesus Christ is committed to fulfilling his plan of redemption in us.

As the late missionary Jim Elliot said, "He is no fool who gives up what he cannot keep in order to gain what he cannot lose."[10] You can never outgive God.

1. How does this passage address Christians today? How does it address you?

_____

2. What are some ways that God has acted in your life following greater commitment to him and greater offering of yourself?

_____

◗ *Pray*

For a renewed church that hungers to give and that sees God's remarkable outflow of his favor.

◗ *Do*

Take God's dare. Give away at least ten percent of your pre-tax income. See what happens.

DAY 16
OUTPOURING OF GRACE

Remember this: Whoever sows sparingly will also reap sparingly, and whoever sows generously will also reap generously.

—2 Corinthians 9:6

◐ Read
2 Corinthians 9:6-10

◐ Apply
God promises that he will pour out even more abundant grace into our lives to the degree that we commit to him. This certainly does not mean that God pays us back. If we give $100 he may not give us $1,000 back, as some people have misunderstood passages like this to mean. But in every instance he gives us (individually and as the church community) something even more precious than himself. Giving builds your relationship with God because, as we've seen already, it builds hope, trust, belief, and commitment to him. The real gain is a closer walk with Jesus Christ, a greater union of your life with his.

Paul also states the converse: whenever Christians, individually or together, hold back, they damage their relationship with Christ. They act without courage; they deny his goodness.

1. The idea of "sowing and reaping" is common in Scripture. Where else does it apply?

2. Do you give because you are motivated that God will reward you in this life somehow? Or does something else motivate your giving?

3. If you were generous, but your financial situation stayed the same (or became even worse), would you stop trusting God? Why or why not?

❍ Pray

For a renewed church that sows generously, with abandon.

❍ Do

To sow generously implies giving until it actually lowers our current lifestyle. What would it take to lower your lifestyle?

DAY 17
ADVENTURE

*"But who am I, and who are my people, that we should be able to
give as generously as this? Everything comes from you, and we
have given you only what comes from your hand..."*

—1 Chronicles 29:14

◗ **Read**
1 Chronicles 29:1-20

◗ **Apply**
David beautifully expresses a heart of gratitude here in
this passage. We too should marvel at even the ability to be
generous. It is one of God's good gifts to us, a sure sign of
our understanding of his grace. Giving to God's kingdom,
laying down our earthly treasures at his feet, has no end. It
is a roller coaster ride through life, an adventure. And yet
it is an adventure that is safe within the loving arms of the
almighty God.

Only the gospel of new life in Christ can sustain such a
life-long experience. To paraphrase G. K. Chesterton: "Every
person wants two things in life: adventure and security. Only
in Christianity do you get both."

1. **Where does your ability to be generous come from? Were you always as generous as you are now, or have you grown in that area?**

2. **How do you live both adventurously and with security as a Christian?**

3. **As a community, how can we live with a greater sense of adventure?**

◗ *Pray*

For a renewed church that recognizes the adventure of the Christian life, the thrill of being a colony of God's people in the world.

◗ *Do*

What is one thing that you are frightened to do for God? Commit to praying for the grace to do that within the next six months. Unite with other Christians (in your fellowship group or friends) to help each other complete your plan.

DAY 18
PLEASING GOD

I have received from Epaphroditus the gifts you sent. They are a fragrant offering, an acceptable sacrifice, pleasing to God. And my God will meet all your needs according to the riches of his glory in Christ Jesus.

—Philippians 4:18b-19

◐ Read
Philippians 4:10-20

◐ Apply
Giving to the work of ministry is really an offering to God himself. When the Philippians gave to Paul, they were actually offering their resources to further God's kingdom. They gave so that his ministry of advancing the claims of the gospel would progress.

All giving is used by God in this way. Money is never meant to be stored up in some type of bank account but instead used for God's kingdom purposes. When the church has hoarded wealth, it has strayed far from God's purposes and needs to repent. He doesn't desire extravagance; he doesn't need worldly success. He is a giving Lord who constantly pours out the "fragrant offerings" given to him back into people so that they would know him.

For example, Paul, the recipient of the Philippians' gift, used that gift to praise God for them. He rejoiced not only for the support, (which he needed), but also for the proof it gave of their changed lives. According to his calling, he used their gift to spread the gospel to even more people.

1. **When you give, do you think of your offering going to God, or just going to "pay the church's bills"?**

2. **What is a better use of God's resources: luxuries or necessities? Why should Christians live a "wartime lifestyle" instead of a "comfort lifestyle"?** [11]

○ *Pray*

For a renewed church that constantly gives out as much as it receives, based on the needs of people surrounding the church.

○ *Do*

Pick something of your own that someone has given to you (not that thing you keep in the back of your closet!) and give it to someone who needs it.

DAY 19
COMMUNITY OF CARE

All the believers were together and had everything in common. They sold property and possessions to give to anyone who had need. Every day they continued to meet together in the temple courts. They broke bread in their homes and ate together with glad and sincere hearts, praising God and enjoying the favor of all the people. And the Lord added to their number daily those who were being saved.

—Acts 2:44-47

● Read
Acts 2:42-47

● Apply
The first Christians instinctively knew that their possessions needed to be shared with their brothers and sisters in Christ. Why? They had seen Jesus live in the same way.

This radical unselfishness stood out as much to the people of their time as it would to modern people. Such an astounding display of generosity and mutual care, mixed with the wonders of the Holy Spirit, pierced the hearts of many.

Giving changes the world. There is no more powerful evidence of the transformation of the gospel than radical generosity.

1. Most people feel that modern Christians could never share their possessions like the Christians in Acts 2. Is that true? Why or why not?

2. In a world where some philanthropists give away millions to charitable causes (often for the fame and recognition it receives), how generous would "ordinary" Christians have to be to catch the attention of the world?

3. How could our giving bring attention to Jesus instead of ourselves?

○ *Pray*

For a renewed church that is so generous that the whole city would notice.

○ *Do*

As you read biographies of Christians, notice how generous they were (or weren't). Try to explain how their use of money fit into their lives as a whole.

DAY 20
PRAISE TO GOD

You will be enriched in every way so that you can be generous on every occasion, and through us your generosity will result in thanksgiving to God.

—2 Corinthians 9:11

◎ Read
2 Corinthians 9:11-15

◎ Apply
When we can bless others with our generosity, the praise goes to God. People who receive the generous grace of Christians are able to praise God "because of the surpassing grace God has given" (verse 14). They know that such a financial gift comes from an even greater source—the grace of God in Jesus Christ.

Giving is just a part of a lifestyle of generosity. Christians always give of their heart, their time, their hope, and their prayers. As we close this 20-day study of biblical stewardship, we reflect on all the different ways that we can give of ourselves.

Jesus died for us to set us free from this life of death. By putting to death the old, we take on the new life found in Christ. We trust that God will provide us the strength to be content in all situations (see Philippians 4:11-13) so that we can in turn sacrifice joyfully for the sake of the gospel.

1. Are you content enough in all situations to willingly be generous "on every occasion"?

2. How does giving of your financial resources encourage greater giving of your whole life to God?

3. Looking back, what has been the greatest lesson that you've learned? How do you think and act differently toward God?

O *Pray*
For a renewed church, full of people with renewed hearts, that is free to risk everything for the sake of the gospel.

O *Do*
Look for other books on Christian stewardship to continue growing in your understanding.

NOTES

1 Idea from *Firstfruits: Managing the Master's Money*, Lillian V. Grissen (Orland Park, Ill: Barnabas Foundation, 1992).

2 Adapted from an idea in *Firstfruits.*

3 "Money and the Meaning of Life: An Interview With Jacob Needleman," Michael Malone. *Fast Company*, June/July 1997.

4 *Matthew: IVP New Testament Commentary*, Craig Keener (Downers Grove, Ill: IVP, 1997) Comment on Matthew 6:24.

5 *Behind the Stained Glass Windows: Money Dynamics in the Church*, John and Sylvia Ronsvalle (Grand Rapids, Mich: Baker, 1996).

6 Statistic from *New York Times* research quoted in "Why The Devil Takes Visa," Rodney Clapp. *Christianity Today*, October 7, 1996.

7 The NIV translates "unrighteous" in this verse as "worldly," which somewhat weakens the point of Christ's claim.

8 *The Challenge of the Disciplined Life*, Richard Foster (New York: HarperSan Francisco, 1985), 53.

9 Ron Voss, quoted in: *Behind the Stained Glass Windows: Money Dynamics in the Church*, John and Sylvia Ronsvalle (Grand Rapids, Mich: Baker, 1996).

10 Jim Elliot quoted in Ronald Blue, "How to Have More Money To Give," *Money for Ministries*, edited by Wesley K. Willmer (Wheaton, Ill: Victor Books, 1989).

11 Adapted from a study guide question by John Piper based on "Money: The Currency of Christian Hedonism," Chapter Five of *Desiring God* (Sisters, Ore: Multnomah Press, 1996).

Go deeper in your study on the topic of generosity.

Generosity: Responding to God's Radical Grace in Community

A Seven-Session Study Guide
by Redeemer Presbyterian Church

(978-1-944549-00-8)

Generosity: How God's Radical Grace Makes Us Givers

A Seven-Part Sermon Series
from Timothy Keller & Abraham Cho

DVD set (978-1-944549-02-2)

Also available on CD (978-1-944549-03-9)

For more information on the Generosity series and other items
related to generosity, visit **gospelinlife.com/generosity**.

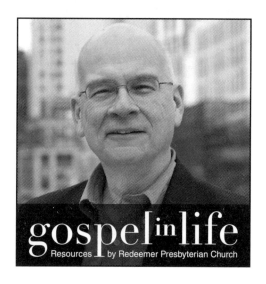

We invite you to visit gospelinlife.com where you can browse 25 years of sermons and resources by Timothy Keller and the staff of Redeemer Presbyterian Church.

View the 10 most popular sermon series:
www.GospelinLife.com/Top10

This list includes a nine-part series on marriage from Ephesians 5, which was the basis for the best-selling book *The Meaning of Marriage*.